"The Movie Making Process"
Using the *process* of making a movie for community engagement
and as an experiential learning tool
"Guerilla Filmmaking with a *Hollywood* Flair" DVD is available on
Amazon.com

This manual is now part of a 4-hour in-service law enforcement class on
crisis intervention, and POST certified in Minnesota.

Original Pilot Project Sponsored by:
The National Alliance on Mental Illness (NAMI) of the St. Croix Valley
and
The Pierce County WI Criminal Justice Coordinating Council (CJCC)

Special thanks to:
Peter VanDusartz III, MA, LCSW, ICS, SAC
Director of Clinical Counseling & Social Services
Manager of Programs for Change at Hudson Hospital and Clinic, Hudson, WI

Sgt. Jeff Kennett, CIT Officer, St. Croix County WI Sheriff's Department

Eric Anderson, Chippewa Valley Technical College, Eau Claire, WI

Linda Flanders, Project Director, CEO Taproot, Inc.

Denise Hackel, President, NAMI St. Croix Valley, WI

River Falls, WI Public Library

Local Community Actors

Partial funding for the pilot-project was generously provided by:

The United Way of Goodhue, Wabasha, and Pierce Counties 2014 Health Grant
The Pierce Pepin Collaborative 2013 Grant
Donation from TurningPoint for Victims of Domestic and Sexual Violence, River Falls, WI
Taproot, Inc. Pierce County, WI and Goodhue County, MN

DE-ESCALATION
SKILLS

2014

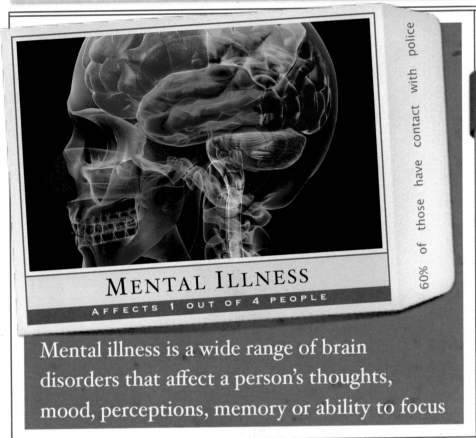

MENTAL ILLNESS
AFFECTS 1 OUT OF 4 PEOPLE

60% of those have contact with police

Mental illness is a wide range of brain disorders that affect a person's thoughts, mood, perceptions, memory or ability to focus

CAUSES OF MENTAL ILLNESS

The diagnosis and treatment of mental illness is based on the signs and symptoms a person is exhibiting, as well as how much the condition affects the person's ability to function in everyday life.

Mental illness can be caused by **biological, psychological** or **environmental** factors.

Biological: This includes brain defects or injury, heredity and genetics, hormones, infections, pre-natal damage, the abnormal balance of chemicals in the brain, or any other unusual brain development.

Psychological: This can be caused by early childhood neglect, or an important early loss, as that of a parent. It can also be caused from any severe psychological trauma: emotional, physical or sexual abuse, or a traumatizing incident.

Environmental: This can occur from exposure to toxins, poor nutrition, substance abuse or chronic stressors: poverty, anxiety, violence, etc.

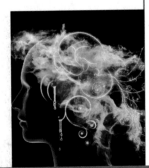

MENTAL HEALTH

Learning Goals

A Brain Disorder

or Chemical Imbalance
Understand a mental illness is a brain disorder or a chemical imbalance. It is not related to intelligence or a defect of character.

Medical Crisis

A Person Needs Your Help
Recognize that a person in a mental health crisis is in a medical crisis and needs your help.

Develop Verbal Skills

for De-escalation
Develop the verbal de-escalation skills you can use with people in a mental health crisis.

Local Resources

and Community Assistance
Discover local mental health resources in Pierce County that can help you on mental health crisis calls.

Living With a Mental Illness

One in four people in the United States has a diagnosable mental illness. That is more than 57.7 million people. Less than one third of them receive treatment.

Of those 57.7 million, 60% or more will come in contact with law enforcement. A 2014 report shows that there are 10 times more people in jail and prison with a severe mental illness than there are in psychiatric hospitals. (*Treatment Advocacy Center*) Over 50% of students with a mental illness drop out of school.

Treatment is essential. Most people with a mental illness, who receive treatment and are stabilized, live long and productive lives. Mother Teresa, Robert Downey Jr., Robin Williams, and Michael Phelps are a few examples of people living with a mental illness, and still are respected and admired for who they are and what they have accomplished.

What Mental Illness is NOT: There is still a stigma against mental illness that does not exist in the world of a physical medical disorder, injury or

A person in a mental health crisis is often scared and confused. An officer who can verbally calm the situation helps everyone, making the situation safer and taking less time in the long-run.

illness. Mental illness is NOT a defect of character. It is NOT a matter of willpower. It is NOT related to intelligence. In fact, many people of superior intelligence experience a mental illness at height of their most productive years. And, while mental illness is a huge issue in the United States, it is also a global epidemic. Mental illness is NOT particular to race, religion, gender or financial situation.

MENTAL ILLNESS

Can Affect Anyone

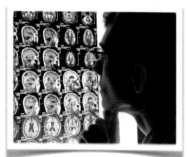

Remember, a mental health crisis is a medical crisis. The behavior is because of a brain disorder or chemical imbalance. As a first responder, remember the MORE stressful the situation, the MORE exaggerated the symptoms.

The Most Common Mental Disorders

While there are different complexities to each mental illness, *and there are many different forms of a mental illness,* there are several mental disorders and their symptoms that you will encounter as a first responder to a crisis call:

- **Anxiety Disorders**
- **Depression**
- **Bipolar Disorder**
- **Schizophrenia**
- **Personality Disorders**
- **Substance Use Disorder that is "co-occurring" with a mental illness**

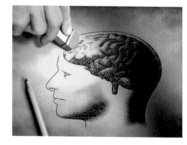

MOST COMMON MENTAL HEALTH DISORDERS

Anxiety Disorders

Anxiety is a normal reaction to stress. When anxiety is excessive , with an irrational dread of everyday situations, it becomes a disabling disorder. This includes Obsessive Compulsive Disorder, Panic Disorder, Post-Traumatic Stress Disorder and other Social Phobias. With soldiers coming home from the Middle East, transitioning back to everyday life can be hard. You may get more crisis calls regarding Post-traumatic Stress.

Depression

More than grief or situational sadness, chronic depression interferes with daily life, causing physical pain and even a form of temporary paralysis. Taking a shower or even eating breakfast becomes an overwhelming activity. A person loses any and all interest in life. They do less, think less and feel less, becoming numb to life. Most people with chronic depression need medical help to get better.

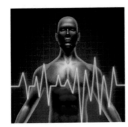

Bipolar Disorder

Everyone has moods, the ups and downs of life, but this is <u>severe</u> ups and downs, with often "out-of-control" behavior. The Manic phase keeps thoughts racing and offers God-like confidence. Speech &movements are very rapid and people have difficulty focussing. Often people cannot, or do not sleep. Mood swings come in cycles. Depressive phases can become suicidal.

Schizophrenia

Thoughts and beliefs are not based on reality. People often see things others don't, or have their attention diverted to voices they hear. They exhibit disorganized speech and motor behavior. Strings of words are put together that rhyme or don't make sense. Posture can look bizarre or people can move with childlike silliness. A person living with schizophrenia needs to focus on you and have attention drawn back into the present. Avoid feeding into hallucinations or delusions.

"People who experience mental health problems are more than three times more likely to have drug problems. Six out of ten addicts have at least one co-occurring mental disorder."

Dr. Nora Volkow
National Institute on Drug Abuse

Personality Disorders

Most Common

This is a pattern of behavior that deviates from universally appropriate behavior: <u>Anti-social</u>, (lack of remorse, putting others at risk, habitual lying) <u>Avoidant</u>, (**extreme** shyness or sensitivity or feelings of inadequacy) or <u>Borderline</u> personality disorder. (pervasive instability in moods, relationships and/or behavior)

Substance Use Disorder.......

Genetics

Genes are the blueprint for a host of traits, behavior and the architecture of brain cells. The genetic component of addiction cannot be overemphasized. Some people are simply more vulnerable.

Trauma

Physical, emotional and sexual abuse are risk factors for later drug use. Trauma can be from a single event or it can occur over the course of years. Trauma occurs when the ability to cope is overwhelmed by the experience.

....Co-occurring with a Mental Illness

Self-medicate

Many people with a mental illness attempt to cover up the symptoms with drug use. It's an attempt to change one's mind state from negative to positive in the short term

Need for Professional Assessment:

Is drug use covering up a mental illness or is the use of drugs causing symptoms of mental illness? It requires a professional assessment to sort it out. Over 90% of people on probation in Pierce County have a dual-diagnosis of mental illness and substance abuse.

Remember a Mental Health Crisis is a Medical Crisis

When responding to a mental health crisis call, it's essential to remember that the more stressful the situation for the person in crisis, the **more exaggerated** the symptoms of the illness.

Avoid Power Struggles: Arguing with someone in a mental health crisis does not work, and can make the situation worse. Reason also does not work well, in a mental health crisis the person is obviously not using reason, nor able to respond to it. A person in crisis also does not necessarily know their behavior is inappropriate: it is up to an officer to explain what is acceptable behavior and what is not. Offer acceptable choices.

Communicate Clearly: While it is essential to explain to a person in crisis what is expected of them, remember to use LESS words when communicating. Speak slowly, as a person's perceptions are distorted while in a crisis and understanding what you say will take longer.

Explain to a person in crisis what you are going to do BEFORE you actually do it. Speak to them in simple words they will understand, and avoid using police jargon or acronyms.

Force Equals Stress: A person in crisis who is forced onto the ground, forced into restraints, or forced into the back of a police car will be be more stressed out and more out of control.

Behavior is from a brain disorder or chemical imbalance: STRESS EXAGGERATES the symptoms.

Reduce stress, reduce the symptoms.

"A person with an anxiety disorder can be irritable, impatient and panic easily. They might worry excessively, and exhibit rapid heartbeat or shortness of breath"

You can help reduce their anxiety...

ANXIETY DISORDERS

18%

Anxiety disorders are the most common mental illnesses and over 18% of Americans are affected by them.

20% of people with anxiety disorders also use drugs to help mask the feelings and get temporary relief. In the long run, illicit drugs worsen the condition of an already malfunctioning neurological system.

SIGNS AND SYMPTOMS of the three conditions officers most likely encounter

Depression: The threat of suicide is very real to those suffering from severe chronic depression. On a crisis call, it is essential to get to the stage where you can ask, "Do you have thoughts of killing yourself?" Observations you can look for are "self-neglect" of not eating or showering, excessive sleeping and a *flat* facial expression. There might be use of drugs or alcohol to cover the symptoms, or great difficulty in concentrating or making decisions. There might be past suicidal attempts or talk of suicide. Most often there are feelings and talk about guilt, worthlessness or hopelessness.

Schizophrenia: You might get a call of a person wandering/or homeless and acting very strange. The most visible signs you will see are a person hearing voices or seeing delusions that others can't hear or see. But they are very real to the person experiencing them. They might have very disorganized speech patterns and put together words that make no sense. A person might exhibit very childlike silliness or bizarre posture.

It's hard to ask "the question" about suicidal thinking. It's not something to rush into, but it does have to be asked. Asking only, "Do you plan to hurt yourself" is not enough. Many people thinking of /or planning suicide have no intention of hurting themselves. They might be thinking of ending their lives quickly and painlessly. "The Question" needs to be asked very specifically.

When speaking to someone with schizophrenia, they might act withdrawn and offer little or no eye contact. They might have a flat affect or speak in a monotone. They lack the ability to begin or sustain any planned activity.

It is often challenging to gain and keep their attention if they are having hallucinations or delusions. It's important to be creative in ways to capture their attention back to the present moment. REMEMBER to not feed into or respond to their hallucinations or delusions.

Risk taking behavior is dangerous or careless actions coupled with an unrealistic belief in one's abilities.

Bi-Polar Disorder: Manic Episode

The depressive phase of Bi-Polar will be similar to the above description. The Manic Episode is the opposite: A very sharp increase in energy and little need or interest in sleep. A person may be very irritable or jumpy, and appear "wired." Thoughts will be racing and speech is very fast. People are easily distracted. The mood will be euphoric and the feeling that life is incredible. "Anything is possible and I can do it all." Most often there will be denial that anything is wrong.

The manic phase is often associated with risk taking behavior, unrealistic beliefs in one's own abilities and careless or poor judgement. Risk taking behavior can include spending sprees, use of drugs or insatiable need for sex.

Not Diagnosed

Mental illnesses exist on a spectrum. Most mental disorders can be easy to miss. We can walk by someone at the grocery store without knowing that the person is living with depression.

In most cases, mental illness is a hidden problem, which makes it harder to fight. Bringing it out of the shadows is a good first step. We can end the stigma.

Not Aware of Disability
Too often we focus only on a person's behavior and believe that the person can "choose" to act that way or not. We fail to recognize that mental illness is a brain disorder.

Assessment and accurate diagnosis is the only way recognize a mental illness.

Not Taking Medication

While medication is not the only means of treating a mental illness, it is the primary way to stabilize brain chemistry. This is often a complex, costly and unpleasant regime. Other times people can feel good, healthy and normal, believing they can discontinue medication.

Taking Medication Incorrectly

Confusion can often cause a person to take an incorrect dose of a prescription medication. A forgotten dose one day could lead to doubling the dose the next day. Others might resist the idea that the condition is chronic and they do not want to be dependent on

Showing Side Effects of Medication

Many people do not like the side effects of the medication. Some experience dry mouth, itchy skin, low sex drive or the feeling of a foggy mind.

It can make people feel like they are "flatlining", having no ups and downs of daily life, but instead feel little emotion at all.

Some gain a large amount of weight very quickly and the medication changes their metabolism.

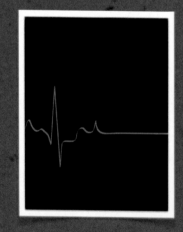

Some people can get worse on medication

Coping

Anyone can end up in a crisis when they are unable to cope with external or internal stressors.

Trauma

Abuse
Childhood trauma upsets the human developmental framework. Trauma can be cumulative with multiple events building upon one another in a negative way that affects how the brain develops.

Violence
Sustained exposure to trauma or violence can develop a variety of negative coping skills in response to traumatic stress, affecting emotional, behavioral, physiological and cognitive functioning.

Substance Abuse

Illicit
Approximately 50 million people in the US suffer from one or more mental illnesses. One third of those develop a substance abuse problem. Many are trying to self-medicate their symptoms.

Prescription
While the proper medication/s for a diagnosed mental illness can be very beneficial, a person who takes too much or too little can exhibit crisis behaviors.

Other Medical Conditions

Brain Injury
A traumatic brain injury can occur even from an injury that is perceived as minor, but causes a distinct change in behavior and brain chemistry.

Alzheimer's or Dementia
In older adults you might find they have lost memory, the ability to plan or organize, or word finding abilities. This group is often the most vulnerable.

MENTAL HEALTH CRISIS
Preliminary Things to Consider

PEOPLE IN CRISIS

WILL HAVE DISTORTED PERCEPTIONS

SLOW DOWN SPEAK SLOWLY

A person is unable to cope
with external or internal stressors.

Safety First

Awareness

Your safety is top consideration. Be aware of your exits and remove potentially dangerous items and casual observers when possible. Recognize how children will be affected by the interaction.

Distance

Keep a safe physical distance and don't take unnecessary risks. At the same time, recognize when the interaction changes and you can increase rapport.

Distortion

A person in crisis will have distorted perceptions. Thoughts speed up or are disjointed. Sounds slow down as will understanding or comprehension.

Taking Longer

Everything will take longer Keep it simple: avoid talking too much, don't shout orders and avoid moving too quickly. EXPLAIN what you are going to do before you do it.

Use of Force

Avoid it as a first choice if possible People in crisis can display extraordinary strength....avoid physical confrontation if possible. Officer safety is key, but avoid a *premature* use of force. People with a history of abuse or victimization may have trauma re-activated by use of force.

HOW DOES THE PERSON APPEAR?

It is not up to you, a law enforcement officer, to diagnose someone in a mental health crisis. However, as a first responder, you do have the ability to notice and document how a person APPEARS, what they are DOING and what they are SAYING.

Does the person appear confused? Do they appear to be having delusions or hallucinations? Do they look afraid or suicidal. Identifying what you see helps you assess the situation and offers concrete information to share in a report. Does the person appear in physical pain or under the influence? Are they highly agitated or appear to be having a flashback? In what way?

What a person says or does also helps in the assessment. Is a person talking, acting or dressing inappropriately? Are they seeing or hearing things that others cannot hear or see? Are they having difficulty focussing on the situation?

What a person says also helps you assess the situation. "It hurts too much, I just want it all to end," or, "I have a meeting with Brad and Angelina", or "They're listening to everything I say and trying to control how I think."

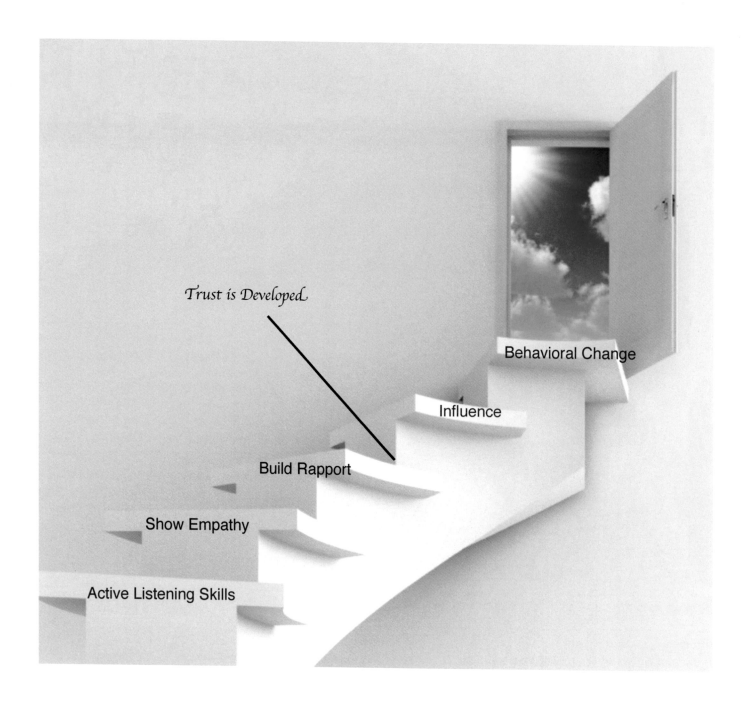

Fuselier Behavioral Change Stairway

From Crisis Intervention Team Training Manual

Communication Skills for Resolving Conflict
Dr. Dwayne Fuselier, FBI Crisis Negotiation Team

Become an ACTIVE LISTENER
Show You Understand a Person's Feelings

Learning to become an **active listener** is a life-long skill that can be used in any situation: from a crisis situation, to personal or professional relationships, to raising children. It means allowing a person to vent their feelings, *not interrupting*, and showing them you are paying attention.

Let the person know you are listening, but be brief in your responses. "Yes", "O.K." or simply, "Go on....." Look directly at the person who is talking, lean forward when possible and use body language that shows the person has your complete attention.

Use Open-Ended Questions that allow for more description. Encourage a person to clarify what they are saying. "Tell me more about that," or "what happened when you..." These types of open ended questions can get deeper into what is really happening and why it is happening right now. Questions that only get you a *yes or no* answer can slow the process and force you to guess about what is happening or how someone is feeling.

Emotional Labeling means you have picked up the clues of the conversation and understood. Use your senses and relate the senses to the emotion: "I can <u>hear anger</u> in your voice "....or "You <u>look sad</u>, how can I help."

Feeling understood is a basic human desire.

Paraphrasing what a person says shows that you really are listening and that you understand the situation. It means repeating back to a person their concerns and feelings, but putting it in your own words. It's an accurate shared understanding of the situation.

This does require that you have actually been paying attention and have picked up the subtle clues of what's being said to be able to put it into a logical context. A person who is ranting about being poisoned by "them" could be someone feeling the effects of chemotherapy.

Use **Effective Pauses** to encourage a person to say more. It's human nature to fill a void. Remaining quiet allows a person in crisis more time to respond to your questions. AVOID talking too much or using long, run-on sentences. You will make things more confusing for the person.

Mirroring What Is Said and Reflective Listening

Mirroring means to repeat the <u>last words</u> a person says. This is another way to show that you are really listening. If someone says, "They're listening to everything I say".....you repeat back the last part......*listening to everything you say.*

Reflective Listening means to echo back exactly what a person has said, the entire sentence. "The government is listening to everything I say." You actually repeat the exact sentence: *The government is listening to everything you say.*

Reflective Meaning is slightly different. Rather than repeating *exactly* what the person is saying, you repeat back to the person in your own words, focusing on **what** happened and how the person **feels.** "You got fired from your job and your roommate told you to move out. You feel angry and afraid about what is gong to happen to you."

Using "I" statements can help personalize you to another person.
"I'm here because I care."

The Blythe Bridge crosses over the divided highway three hundred feet below. A teenage girl is sitting on the railing of the bridge, kicking her feet out and back like on a swing. Risky. The breeze is blowing her hair and she has her face tilted up towards the sun.

Lunch is so close I can already picture the sandwich and…

I look up, suddenly cut out from my own mind seeing a kid sitting on the edge of the bridge above me. *(Ah fuck.)* I cut it sharp, across the lanes, nearly missing the ramp. *(Sometimes I really do love this job.)* As I pull off onto the shoulder, I call it in, reaching down for the radio and unable to look away from the kid.

"You want help out there, John?" They ask me.

"Naw, she's just a kid."

"Right. 10-4"

I get out of the car I walk slow, I don't want to frighten her, but can't come across as condescending either. *(If she falls…)* As though she knows I'm here, she looks down between her feet at the road so far away. My stomach falls through to my own feet. *(Oh no….Don't fucking do it…)* I don't run, but I pick up my pace. My heart beats loud enough to hear in my own ears. With the sound of my footsteps she turns suddenly to face me. Her eyes are red, tears streaming down her cheeks and her face is all blotchy.

"**Stay away! I'll jump.** Stay away and leave me alone."

I freeze, my heart seems to follow suit, but nevertheless I reach cautiously for my radio.

"Don't move and stay away from me!" She yells again.

I drop my hand, nodding, doing my best to seem as friendly as humanly possible. The smile on my face feels strained. "Hi, my name's John. I'll stay right here. I'm here to help."

"You can't help me."

I let the comment pass. "Can you tell me your name?" I don't get any response, simply a look of equal parts fear and misery.

"I don't think I know you."

"Nobody knows me," she says. I wait.

"Abbey, my name's Abbey."

"Abbey, tell me what's wrong. What's happened?"

No response, just feet dangling, swaying in the wind that seems to only grow faster.

"Abbey, no one is ever beyond help."

No response.

(OK, something else maybe.) "Abbey, how did you get here?"

Blythe Bridge
Active Listening Skills Con't

Nothing at first, then a soft whisper almost lost in the wind. "I walked. I walked and I walked. And guess what? I walked some fucking more."

I start to slowly edge forward, step by step. Inching.

"Would you come off the railing, at least for a moment, so we can talk?"

"Don't come near me! Stay back. You can't help me!"

I freeze in my tracks again. *(Fuck!)* "Abbey I can see you're upset. I do want to help. Tell me more about how you walked and ended up here?"

There was silence for a moment before she began speaking again. "I wanted to walk to the end of the earth....or just walk to… to the end. And I found it. This is the end....Blythe Bridge.....the beginning and the end....... My parents drove across this bridge the night I was born. Getting over to Regions Hospital........ Makes sense, doesn't it? The beginning and the end. Poetic."

She laughed humorlessly. Desperate, I rack my mind searching for the right words. *(OK, when in doubt John, repeat back...)*

"OK, so you crossed over this bridge the night you were born. Can you tell me more about how you got here tonight? I can tell you're hurting, what happened to make you feel this is the end?"

I get no response save the turn of a shoulder as she again looked down at the highway below.

(OK, too much....ease up John)

"Abbey, what happened tonight that makes you feel like it's the end?"

Nothing for a moment… but than something. The first inklings of an explanation perhaps.

"**My parents told me** to get out. They said… they hated me."

She looks away again, her eyes gleaming over with a glaze I found terrifying.

"Abbey, please, tell me more"

"They said I was… an abomination."
"So you feel your parents hate you. You're not alone in that Abbey. At the

best of times, being a teenager is hard."

"I told them I was gay."

I stay quiet, I'm out of my comfort zone on this one. I'm hoping she'll say more.

"I told them I was gay and they told me to get out. They wouldn't let me live there if I *chose* to be gay."

I could feel myself holding my breath, the beat of my heart was booming again. *(Breathe John, breathe. Let her see you taking some deep breaths.)*

"**Do I understand** this right? You told your parents you're gay, and they said you couldn't live there anymore? So you walked to this bridge and now you feel this is the end? You… don't want to live anymore?"

"Yes. As long as I *chose* to be gay, I'm a freak. They don't want a freak living with them. They say it as though it's a choice. What choice? I don't remember anyone giving me a choice! They're…they're fucking idiots." *(OK...this is progress. She's talking.)*

"**Well I'm here** because I care. I want to help you…a lot of people are gay, Abbey. A lot of good hearted, hard-working, talented people are gay."

"Not if they're Catholic they're not. Not in *motherfucking* Michigan."

SHOWING EMPATHY
Putting Yourself in Another's Shoes

Empathy is the ability to understand a person's feeling and motivation for the behavior. Is there something in your own life that can give you a sense of what another is going through? We do not have to condone behavior, we are asking ourselves if we can relate in any way? Have we suffered a death of a loved one, lost a job or felt the effects of post traumatic stress?

Seeing a situation from another's perspective: Showing empathy means we are looking at the situation from another person's perspective and thinking, "How would I feel?" Why would we offer more compassion to someone with a kidney disorder than to someone with a brain disorder?

A mental illness is a brain disorder or chemical imbalance, caused by something outside of one's own free will. Showing empathy means to be REAL, be AUTHENTIC and be HONEST.

Weapons: It's essential to understand that the "threat" of using a weapon with a person in a mental health crisis will not work. It will not calm someone down. While officer safety, and the safety of others, is your number one priority, avoid a "premature" showing of weapons when possible. If you take out your taser or baton, be sure you are committed to using them. Verbal De-escalation techniques are designed to be an initial strategy to do just that: De-escalate. Weapons will escalate.

It's not feeling sorry for a person, but instead it means to understand their feelings. This builds trust. Trust builds relationships. A relationship leads to a more positive resolution for everyone.

Tone of voice indicates your attitude. It's essential to be aware of "how" you sound:

Sarcastic vs. Curious

Authoritative vs. Gentle

People in a crisis will respond to the tone of your voice without understanding the meaning.

TONE OF VOICE & BODY LANGUAGE

Body Language

A more primitive part of the brain unconsciously responds to facial expressions and body language.

More so in a crisis than in a day to day interactions, people notice body language and what your facial expression reflects.

Crossing your arms or putting your hands on your hips can be viewed as argumentative or threatening. A person in crisis who feels threatened can escalate the crisis.

Find the fine line where you can be prepared, but also receptive.

Above all: AVOID smirking or laughing at someone. It's disrespectful, shows lack of empathy and can escalate the situation.

Blythe Bridge (Chapter 2: Showing Empathy)

Not if they're Catholic they're not. Not in *motherfucking* Michigan."

(She has me on that one.....OK, keep your voice low and slow John....low and slow) "Abbey, will you come back over on this side of the railing please. Just sit and talk with me a bit?" No response. I keep my hands in front of me so she can see them.

"Abbey?" I take another step forward.

"Stay back!! Stay away from me!" I freeze.

"**I'm perverted,** did you know that? That's what they said, my own father said I was perverted. Maybe they're right.....I don't fit in. I never have."

"You say you never felt like you fit it, what's happened to make you feel like that?" *(I'm talking even softer....she's not going to let me move closer yet, but maybe I can lean against the bridge.)*

She looks over at me, but before she can tell me to stop, "I'm just going to lean against the railing for a bit Abbey." She doesn't say anything, but her eyes are flitting from me to the road below. "What happened to make you feel like you don't fit in?"

"**I have no friends.** I can't tell anyone I'm gay, not in this school. I

think my gym teacher's hotter than any of the boys, and the most exciting day of my life was when I kissed a girl at summer camp when I was twelve. That's pretty pathetic when the best day of your life was when you were 12." I'm looking over at her, but I don't make any more movements. "So you have no friends at school and you realized you were gay when you were 12." *(Just keep repeating back what she says...keep her talking John)*

"**I knew long before that,** but that was the first time I ever kissed a girl. There's nobody at school that thinks

like me. Nobody knows what it's like."

(Relate John, think of something you can relate this to........) "I do know the feeling of not fitting in. When I was 12, I was already 6 feet tall. I weighed about 120 pounds. There was no one who looked like me."

"That's not even close, you aren't gay....you don't know."
(Honesty John, keep it honest) "No, I don't know what it's like to be gay. But I do know what's it's like to have people stare at me, and me feeling like I'm the only person in the world who's this tall and skinny. I know I felt scared much of the time and wondered what was wrong with me." Finally, Abbey looks over at me. I look at her. For a split second, we're on the same page.

She whispers, I can barely hear her.

"Do you know what it feels like to be truly alone?"

BUILDING RAPPORT

Working Toward Desired Change

Connecting with someone in crisis requires the ability to recognize how you might feel in the other person's place. Can you explain to them how and why you might feel the same? The goals to reach are:

• **We want everyone to remain unharmed**

• **Get what help is needed**

• **Solve the problem together**

Concern and Caring

Be consistent. Keep coming back to remind the person of your desire to help. During active listening, you have become aware of their areas of concern. Bring the conversation back to those areas to have a discussion about their concerns. The person is now listening to you, as well as talking. You are developing trust, and TRUST is the turning point to de-escalation.

Ethics

Being respectful is always essential to a person in crisis. Be honest and explain what you are doing, or going to do. Recognize that it is hard to have a difficult/honest discussion about deep and sometimes dark secrets. Talk on a personal level and allow a person to see beyond the uniform. Is there something you can "safely" share with the person to make the conversation more intimate than authoritarian? *Remember to make it real.*

Validation

Feelings are not right or wrong, they just ARE. Feelings come from a more basic part of the brain/ body connection. Let the person know it's OK to feel whatever they are feeling. It's what we do with those feelings that make a difference. However, validation of those feelings MUST ALWAYS come before problem solving and suggesting options for change. Validate the emotions first to get a person's willingness to problem solve or voluntarily decide on options.

Working to develop rapport, being <u>respectful</u> and authentically concerned are essential to verbally de-escalate a mental health crisis. But officer safety is still your number one concern. Be aware. Be prepared to move quickly.

Developing Trust

Two-way communication means you now have a discussion. It includes both verbal and non-verbal means.

Verbal

Honesty

Respond to a person in crisis so they know you heard them. Avoid arguing or reasoning with psychotic thinking. Do not respond to delusions or hallucinations, but accept the other person does experience them. Be honest about what you are going to do and what's happening.

Explanation

Explain procedures before you do them. Speak slowly and in language the other person understands. Create an honest connection, not one of authority.

Non-Verbal

Body Language

Do not touch a person in crisis or invade their space whenever possible. Avoid actions or authoritarian stance that can appear threatening. Do not smirk, show contempt or hostility.

Slow Down

While consciously slowing down what you say, and using pauses, also slow down your movements and gestures. A person in crisis is in a hyper aware state. Explain first, then move slowly.

Aware of Change

Physical Signs

Watch for facial expressions to change from anger or fear to that of curiosity. Look for a person to take in a relaxing breath of air or relax their posture.

Willingness

Is the person willing to sit or allow you to move into the room. Look for any sign of increased willingness to work with you.

Blythe Bridge (Chapter 3: Building Rapport)

Do you know what it feels like to be truly alone?"

I'm about to answer when my radio squawks. "Headquarters, three David two, you still OK out there John?" Abbey's eyes go wide like a deer in the headlights.

(Tell her what's happening John) "I have to answer the radio, Abbey, otherwise they're going to send someone out to check on me. I'm going to slowly reach up to my microphone and tell them to give me another 10 minutes." She just stares at me.

"Three David two copy? .....John?"

I slowly reach up to my shoulder mic. "Yeah, three David two, I'm OK. Give me another ten minutes."

"10-4 John." I slowly bring my hand back down.

(Validate what she's going through, John. Let her know it's OK) "It makes sense you'd feel angry and all alone. It's OK to feel scared. I'd feel scared if I was sitting on the edge of a bridge railing too. Would you come over on this side of the bridge now? We can talk more sitting on this side."

Abbey doesn't respond, but she's still looking at me, not down at the highway. "Have you? Felt all alone?"

(What are you willing to tell her, John?) "Well, I got divorced a few years ago. That was hard.........yeah, I felt all alone. But I wasn't really. I had a support system. I had a couple of guys I could talk to. Other guys who'd been through it and told me I'd come out of it OK."

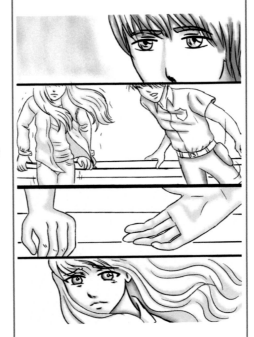

She just stares off. "Abbey, who in your life could be a support system for you?" For a moment I don't think she's going to answer.

"I have a grandmother I like. She lives in Minneapolis. My grandpa's pretty cool too........but I've never told them."

(Prioritize for her, John, prioritize) "It seems like right now, your safety is the biggest issue. And, you're not completely alone, I'm here and I'm not going anywhere."

"How long were you alone? When you got divorced?" *(OK, good, she's asking questions. She's getting curious, like maybe there's another option out there)*

"I was alone for about a year. I dated a couple of times but I wasn't really ready. Now I'm seeing someone I like a lot." She's looking over at me again. "Feeling all alone sucks, Abbey, I know. But it doesn't last. People heal. Hurt feelings heal. You're parents might be scared too. They might not know how to handle a gay daughter. That doesn't mean they don't care. Not really."

"Why do you care?"

"Well, if I had a younger sister, and she was scared, angry and sitting on the edge of a bridge, I'd hope to God someone would stop. I'd hope someone would take her hand.... tell her she's not alone.....I'd hope someone would tell her she matters."

I start to slide sideways, then stop myself. *(Tell her first John, tell her what you're going to do)* "Abbey, I'm going to slide a little closer." I slide over a foot. Then another. I reach out my hand, I can almost touch her.

"Take my hand, Abbey. Come on back over. We'll figure this out. You're not alone......I'm right here."

I reach my hand a bit closer. She lets out the breathe she was holding and takes my hand.

"Come on, come on back over. I've got you." She slowly moves her legs back over to my side of the railing. We both slide down the rails till we're sitting on the ground. I let out the breathe I was holding.

Terra firma never felt so good!

EXERTING INFLUENCE

Without Apparent Force or Authority

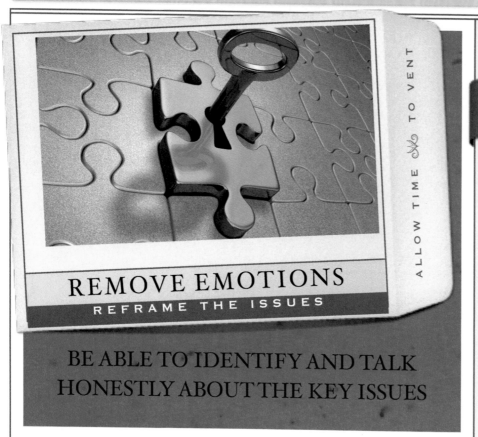

ALLOW TIME TO VENT

REMOVE EMOTIONS
REFRAME THE ISSUES

BE ABLE TO IDENTIFY AND TALK HONESTLY ABOUT THE KEY ISSUES

Offer Options

Priorities

Priority 1

What needs to actually happen right now?

Most Important

What does the person in crisis see as the most important issue?

Past Attempts

What has already been tried? What worked best and was most successful? What didn't work?

Need

What does the person in crisis feel they need?

Available Resources

Family
What family or personal resources are available to the person. What is their support system? Are there friends who could help?

Community
What are the community resources that could be utilized to the person if they are willing to accept help voluntarily? Based upon all the above information, what options can be offered? What option is the person willing to do voluntarily?

A COURSE OF ACTION

Using active listening skills, you have allowed the person to vent their feelings. Using open-ended questions, you have been able to draw out more detailed information. By removing the emotions, you have been able to identify and discuss the key issues. The relationship has now developed to where a person in crisis is willing to respond to your suggestions or offers of help.

Be honest about the options available. If voluntary, there are more local options available. Discuss options and take them to their logical conclusion.

Be clear on options you cannot take. "I cannot leave you alone. We have to find another option." When possible, suggest at least three options for a person to choose from. Three options truly allows for choice. Help the person help you to find a solution.

REMEMBER: If a course of action is suggested prematurely before a relationship is established, the chances of positively overcoming the crisis are **greatly reduced.**

Terra firma never felt so good! Tears are streaming down her face. "What am I going to do?" My heart breaks, she looks so miserable.

"Well, you made the perfect choice. You came back over the rail. You're safe now."

She looks up at me, her eyes glistening. "Yeah, but I'm still gay."

I can't help but smile at this kid. "Well, yeah, there's that." She manages a weak smile....but it's a smile. (*Ask her what she thinks, John*) "What do you feel is the next most important issue, Abbey?"

The smile evaporates. "I have no where to go."

"There are good people in the community. We're not completely without gay resources." The tears start all over again. (*Come up with some options for her John...think...*) "Long term...what about your grandparents? I could call them. Explain the situation"

She grabs my arm. "You can't tell them!!"

"I won't, not until you tell me it's OK." I wait........I'm hoping she'll fill the void, be open to the idea. "If you don't tell them, Abbey, they won't be able to fully understand the situation."

She hangs her head, pulls her knees up and the crying starts for real. (*Walk her through the options, John, take it to its logical conclusion for her.......she's still not thinking straight yet*) "Another option, Abbey, is to tell the truth. We don't know for sure what will happen, but it is the truth so we're starting from a solid place."

She's still crying, but I think she's listening. "Another option is to lie. But then you'd end up in the same uncomfortable situation again, pretending to be someone you're

not......how open minded do you think your grandparents are?"

Abbey wipes her face on her sleeve. She stares off......"I'm not sure. They're better than my parents."

"What do you think their answer might be about you coming to visit for a while? Maybe stay with them?"

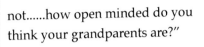

She takes a breath, the blotchy red of her face is beginning to fade. "We have fun. I think they'd be OK with it." She looks right at me. "Will you take me there, John?" Now I'm the one holding my breath. (*Now what are you going to do John? You can't lie to her.*)

The radio takes control. "Headquarters to three David two."

I grab my mic. "Yeah, 3 David 2, I'm on my way in."

"10-4. Copy."

"Come on Abbey, let's walk to the car." She follows me willingly, reaches out and takes my hand. (*Tell her John, be honest, tell her upfront what's going to happen*)

Chapter 4
Exerting Influence

She takes a breath, the blotchy red of her face is beginning to fade. "We have fun. I think they'd be OK with it." She looks right at me. "Will you take me there, John?" Now I'm the one holding my breath. (*Now what are you going to do John? You can't lie to her.*)

The radio takes control. "Headquarters to three David two."

I grab my mic. "Yeah, 3 David 2, I'm on my way in."

kid. "Abbey, it's important to set priorities. I can certainly call your grandparents and see what we can arrange. I can go talk to your parents. I can even find you some support groups, but the very next step is to get you to a professional....so you can talk over what happened today........what lead up to us being here on the bridge."

She jerks her hand away. "I don't want to talk to anyone else!" (*Oh fuck, here we go*)

"You know I mean someone more professional than me."
She looks so scared. She just whispers, "I know what you're talking about....a hospital."

"Yeah, a hospital." She doesn't respond, just keeps kicking the dirt. But she leans against the car and takes a big breath. (*Give her space John. Give her some time to think it through*) Slowly she lifts her head up to look at me.

"10-4. Copy."

"Come on Abbey, let's walk to the car." She follows me willingly, reaches out and takes my hand. (*Tell her John, be honest, tell her upfront what's going to happen*)

We get to the car, the tears have stopped. She looks like a tired little

We're standing by the car. Abbey kicks the dirt with her feet. "Abbey, I'm sorry, but I don't have an option about this first part. I have to take you to talk to someone."

She doesn't look up, just keeps kicking dirt. "I'm talking to you."

"Will I have to stay long?"

BEHAVIOR CHANGE

The person in crisis has calmed to the point of understanding the need for help and agrees to a plan of action.

Set Clear Limits
Reasonable Limits
Enforceable Limits

Person agrees voluntarily to the best option available

Explain Appropriate Behavior and WHY

Talk about areas you both agree on

Stay future oriented

Avoid statements that back people into a corner

Give reasonable choices and consequences

Give the person time to choose one of the options

Give logical consequences, but do not make threats

Enforce the consequences

Make it EASY for the person to agree and take action willingly

---

CRISIS INTERVENTION
Local Resources

National Resources

(Look for State or Local Affiliates)

Advocacy

National Alliance on Mental Health (NAMI)
National Institute of Mental Health
The National Council of Behavioral Health
National Coalition for Mental Health Recovery
American Mental Health Counselors Association
Alcoholics Anonymous
American Foundation for Suicide Prevention
National Center on Domestic Violence, Trauma and Mental Health
Veterans Assistance
Military One Source
Wounded Warrior Project

www.nami.org
www.nimh.nih.gov
www.thenationalcouncil.org
www.ncmhr.org
www.amhca.org
www.aa.org
www.afsp.org

www.nationalcenterdvtraumamh.org
www.mentalhealth.gov
www.militaryonesource.mil
www.woundedwarriorproject.org

Crisis Services

National Suicide Lifeline   800-273-8255

Will I have to stay long?"

(Keep it real....John. Just get ready in case she bolts) "I can't really say Abbey, it's not my call. But I do think that if you can explain to them what you've explained to me, and we have a plan about contacting your parents, grandparents and some support groups for you, then I think they'll see what a smart kid you are. I doubt you'd have to stay long."

"I'm not a kid."

I can't help but smile at her. "No, you're not. Sorry......."

"Where's the hospital? How do I reach my grandparents? Are you going to talk to my parents? I don't want to see them."

"The hospital is on the other side of the county. I can call ahead and tell them we're on our way."

"Then what? Are you just going to drop me off?"

"No, I wouldn't want to just be dropped off either. I'll talk to the doctor. I can call your grandparents and see what we can arrange. I can go talk to your parents and explain." She just stares at me. *(God, she looks so trusting.......don't blow this John)*

"I won't leave you Abbey until we have a plan in place."

She wipes her face again with her sleeve. Takes a deep breathe and says, "OK.... OK, I'll go."

Blythe Bridge Epilogue

I **pull up** to the front of the station, lean over and kiss my wife. *(You're damn lucky John)*

I jump out and she slides over to take the wheel. I look at our sleeping baby in the back seat. *(Don't I know it!)* "Bye babe, see you tonight."

I jog up the steps and into the station. I hit the locker room, trade insults with the guys and suit up. I hook on my gun belt and head out to the briefing room. I swing by and check my mailbox.

I find a large envelop with fancy printed lettering. The return address is Minneapolis. I don't know anyone in Minneapolis.
(I wonder.......?)

I open it up. Inside is a graduation announcement and invitation to a grad party. The picture on the front is beautiful Abbey with shorter hair and carrying a fishing pole. She looks happy. Damn happy.

Across the front of the invitation a magic marker scrawled........THANK YOU.

(You know....I've never been to Minneapolis)

I wonder?

Thank you!!!

TWO free videos accompany this manual:

Introduction to Crisis Intervention

https://youtu.be/-1YCwQ88-LE

Law Enforcement Crisis Intervention De-escalation Steps

https://youtu.be/JERkZoWGLWQ

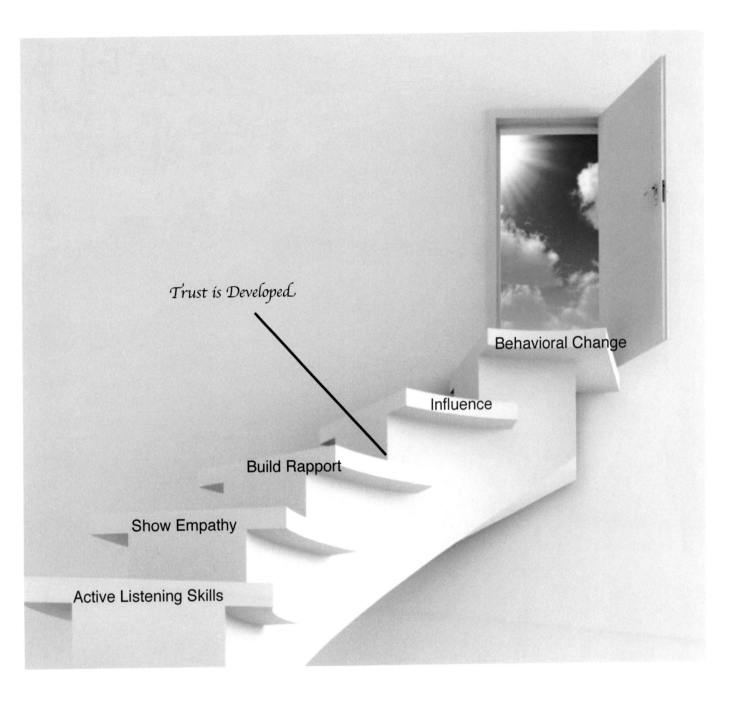

Trust is Developed

Behavioral Change

Influence

Build Rapport

Show Empathy

Active Listening Skills

Fuselier Behavioral Change Stairway

From Crisis Intervention Team Training Manual
Communication Skills for Resolving Conflict
Dr. Dwayne Fuselier, FBI Crisis Negotiation Team

Made in the USA
Middletown, DE
12 August 2017